GROWING OLDER & WISER

9 STUDIES FOR INDIVIDUALS OR GROUPS

LifeGuide®
BIBLE STUDIES

DALE LARSEN
AND SANDY LARSEN

IVP Connect

An imprint of InterVarsity Press
Downers Grove, Illinois

InterVarsity Press
P.O. Box 1400, Downers Grove, IL 60515-1426
ivpress.com
email@ivpress.com

InterVarsity Press® is the book-publishing division of InterVarsity Christian Fellowship/USA®, a movement of students and faculty active on campus at hundreds of universities, colleges and schools of nursing in the United States of America, and a member movement of the International Fellowship of Evangelical Students. For information about local and regional activities, visit intervarsity.org.

LifeGuide® is a registered trademark of InterVarsity Christian Fellowship.

All Scripture quotations, unless otherwise indicated, are taken from the Holy Bible, New International Version®. NIV®. *Copyright ©1973, 1978, 1984 by International Bible Society. Used by permission of Zondervan Publishing House. All rights reserved.*

Cover image: © Vesna Armstrong / Trevillion Images

ISBN 978-0-8308-3044-2

Printed in the United States o f America ∞

P   32   31   30   29

Y   30   29   28   27   26   25   24   23

Contents

Getting the Most Out of *Growing Older & Wiser* —————— 5

1 **Wise Up!** James 1:1-8, 12 ————— 9

2 **Wisdom Hunt** Colossians 2:1-10————— 13

3 **Listening to the Young** Job 32 ————— 17

4 **When the Kids Are Grownups Too** Exodus 18 ————— 21

5 **Wiser by Faith** Genesis 24:1-9 ————— 26

6 **They Don't Always Listen** 1 Kings 12:1-20 ————— 30

7 **A Reason to Be Here** Philippians 1:18-26 ———— 35

8 **Dealing with Fears** Psalm 71:1-13 ————— 40

9 **Lifelong Trust** Psalm 71:14-24 ————— 44

Leader's Notes ————————————— 48

Getting the Most Out of
Growing Older & Wiser

Who wants to get older? Nobody.

Well, maybe some people wish the years would hurry up. There's the fourteen-year-old who longs to be able to drive a car. There's the seventeen-year-old who can't wait to leave home and be independent. There's even the fifty-three-year-old who looks forward to early retirement at fifty-five. After age twenty-five or so, most of us dread those relentlessly accumulating birthdays.

We aren't encouraged by a prevailing culture that treats youth as a divine state where all is beauty, suppleness and freedom. Who would want to outgrow such a place? No wonder older people are often portrayed as a joke, and the prospect of old age seems like a curse. If we can't avoid it, at least we can try to put it off as long as possible.

Not every culture worships youth as ours does. In societies where tradition is vital, older people are venerated as the keepers of history and knowledge. In their view the role of the elders is to pass along the old stories to the young.

Even the most youth-obsessed among us have to admire older people for their sheer endurance. Only a century ago, most people did not "get old and die," instead, most people died young. To reach old age was a mark of God's favor and of the person's fortitude, to have lived through so much and survived.

Today (at least in the West) more and more of us are surviving, and we are surviving longer. Centuries ago the Bible reported that "The length of our days is seventy years—or eighty, if we have the strength" (Psalm 90:10). Now an amazing number of people are living to be one hundred. As we are writing this study guide, people are alive whose lifetimes have spanned the nineteenth, twentieth and twenty-first centuries. Even more remarkable, many of them continue to actively enjoy life.

We have made great strides toward longer, healthier physical lives. We are older, and maybe we are even smarter.

Are we any more wise?

Life expectancies have stretched, but the Bible reveals that human nature has not changed. In the Scripture studies in this book, you will find examples of people who got older and wiser, and examples of people who, well, just got older. You will find older people who should have listened to younger people and vice versa. You will find honest expressions of fear and hope as the years accumulate and death looms closer. Throughout all of these stories you will find the constancy of God.

Whether we consider ourselves "young" or "middle-aged" or "senior citizens" or prefer no age label at all, we will grow wiser as we consider and apply the timeless truths of Scripture. God has made us for himself, and mere physical survival is not our highest goal. No matter how many years we accumulate on this earth, we are offered his gift of eternal life in Christ. May we spend our years here, whether few or many, growing wiser and becoming more like him.

Suggestions for Individual Study

1. As you begin each study, pray that God will speak to you through his Word.

2. Read the introduction to the study and respond to the personal reflection question or exercise. This is designed to help you focus on God and on the theme of the study.

3. Each study deals with a particular passage—so that you can delve into the author's meaning in that context. Read and reread the passage to be studied. The questions are written using the language of the New International Version, so you may wish to use that version of the Bible. The New Revised Standard Version is also recommended.

4. This is an inductive Bible study, designed to help you discover for yourself what Scripture is saying. The study includes three types of questions. *Observation* questions ask about the basic facts: who, what, when, where and how. *Interpretation* questions delve into the meaning of the passage. *Application* questions help you discover the implications of the text for growing in Christ. These three keys unlock the treasures of Scripture.

Write your answers to the questions in the spaces provided or in a personal journal. Writing can bring clarity and deeper understanding of yourself and of God's Word.

5. It might be good to have a Bible dictionary handy. Use it to look up any unfamiliar words, names or places.

6. Use the prayer suggestion to guide you in thanking God for what you have learned and to pray about the applications that have come to mind.

7. You may want to go on to the suggestion under "Now or Later," or you may want to use that idea for your next study.

Suggestions for Members of a Group Study

1. Come to the study prepared. Follow the suggestions for individual study mentioned above. You will find that careful preparation will greatly enrich your time spent in group discussion.

2. Be willing to participate in the discussion. The leader of your group will not be lecturing. Instead, he or she will be encouraging the members of the group to discuss what they have learned. The leader will be asking the questions that are found in this guide.

3. Stick to the topic being discussed. Your answers should be based on the verses which are the focus of the discussion and not on outside authorities such as commentaries or speakers. These studies focus on a particular passage of Scripture. Only rarely should you refer to other portions of the Bible. This allows for everyone to participate in in-depth study on equal ground.

4. Be sensitive to the other members of the group. Listen attentively when they describe what they have learned. You may be surprised by their insights! Each question assumes a variety of answers. Many questions do not have "right" answers, particularly questions that aim at meaning or application. Instead the questions push us to explore the passage more thoroughly.

When possible, link what you say to the comments of others. Also, be affirming whenever you can. This will encourage some of the more hesitant members of the group to participate.

5. Be careful not to dominate the discussion. We are sometimes so eager to express our thoughts that we leave too little opportunity for others to respond. By all means participate! But allow others to also.

6. Expect God to teach you through the passage being discussed and through the other members of the group. Pray that you will have an enjoyable and profitable time together, but also that as a result of the study you will find ways that you can take action individually and/or as a group.

7. Remember that anything said in the group is considered confidential and should not be discussed outside the group unless specific permission is given to do so.

8. If you are the group leader, you will find additional suggestions at the back of the guide.

1

Wise Up!

Pain raises difficult questions. Why is this happening to me? Did I do something wrong? Is God angry with me? How long will this last? Should I pray for instant relief, or should I tough it out?

When we hurt, what we want most is deliverance; God says that what we need most is wisdom. If we let God work his purposes, he will enable us to grow and mature through the difficulties that come into our lives.

GROUP DISCUSSION. What is the difference between being smart and being wise?

PERSONAL REFLECTION. Who is the wisest person you know (or have ever known)? Why do you consider that person wise?

James, Jesus' half-brother, wrote to persecuted Christians throughout the Roman Empire. He wrote before A.D. 50 when the church was still very young. Believers barely knew what it meant to be Christians, and now they had to learn to be Christians under trial. *Read James 1:1-8, 12.*

---

1. James writes that we should "count it pure joy" when we face "trials of many kinds" (v. 2). What is your gut-level response to that advice?

---

2. How does James justify his seemingly outlandish words (vv. 3-4)?

---

3. What is the connection between wisdom and perseverance?

---

4. What is one thing you have learned through difficult experiences?

---

5. How would you describe a spiritually mature and complete person (v. 4)?

6. Do you think anyone gets to such a state of maturity in this life? Why or why not?

7. In what spirit should believers pray for wisdom (vv. 5-8)?

8. How would you define a double-minded person (v. 8)?

9. A Christian who prays in difficult circumstances is bound to have fleeting thoughts such as, *This won't work* or *God won't answer me.* Do you believe this is the sort of doubt to which James refers in verses 6-8? Why or why not?

10. What external or internal pressures tempt you to be double-minded?

11. Verse 12 promises a heavenly reward for those who persevere. What benefits does perseverance also provide in this life?

---

12. What trials is God using right now to build your perseverance?

---

13. How would you like to respond to those trials in a more mature way?

Pray that you will trust God to work out his purposes in any trials you are now experiencing. Boldly ask for joy in the certainty that he is using your problems to make you a more mature Christian.

Now or Later

Where do you especially need wisdom from the Lord? Reread James 1:6. Draw yourself on a small raft riding on wind-tossed ocean waves. Label the "waves" (and, if appropriate, the "raft"). In the spirit of James 1:5, write a prayer for wisdom. Draw yourself again, this time in a sturdy boat on a placid body of water, or if you dislike boats, draw yourself safe on land!

Study Philippians 3:7-16 and/or 2 Peter 1:3-11 with a focus on how maturity in Christ produces Christlike character.

2

Wisdom Hunt

Colossians 2:1-10

Advice columnists, talk-show hosts, commercials, infomercials. We have no shortage of people telling us how to live. With breathtaking authority, even arrogance, they proclaim to us their version of the truth.

As we drown in this flood of opinions and pseudoinformation, we ask what Job asked a long time ago: "Where can wisdom be found?" (Job 28:12). Scripture tells us that wisdom is hidden, but it is hidden where anyone who seeks can find it.

GROUP DISCUSSION. Suppose you find a map to a buried treasure not far from your home. The map does not reveal the nature of the treasure. What would you do? Who would you tell? Who would you not tell? What would you hope the treasure turned out to be?

PERSONAL REFLECTION. What is the best discovery you ever made? How did it happen? How did it change your life?

Christians in the Gentile city of Colossae had come under the influence of Gnostic teachers who claimed that Jesus Christ was insufficient for salvation. These teachers offered a secret knowledge that promised to take Christians to another level. Paul wrote to encourage the Colossian believers to trust in Christ alone for salvation. *Read Colossians 2:1-10.*

1. How would you sum up Paul's intentions for the Christians in Colossae and Laodicea? Note particular words and phrases that lead you to your answer.

2. When have you heard it said or implied that, in order to be saved, you needed "Jesus plus . . ."? What was the "plus"?

3. In what sense is Christ "the mystery of God" (v. 2)?

4. Paul makes the remarkable claim that *all* the treasures of wisdom and knowledge are hidden in Christ (v. 3). When you consider the many branches of human knowledge—for example physics, biology, mathematics, history—in what sense do you think Paul could make this claim?

5. Why was Paul pleased with reports about the Colossian church (v. 5)?

6. What will ensure the Colossians' continued spiritual growth—as well as ours (vv. 6-8)?

7. In contemporary society what are some hollow and deceptive ideas that compete with Christ (v. 8)?

8. When and how have you been taken in by a false idea, and how did you eventually see through it?

9. Paul proclaims two "fullnesses" in verses 9-10. How are the two fullnesses related?

10. How does the fullness in verse 9 assure that our fullness in Christ is complete?

11. Where do you feel inadequate to discern truth from falsehood?

12. How can this passage from Colossians equip you to exercise discernment?

Thank God that Christ has provided all we need for salvation. Pray that you will stay rooted in him and will not be deceived by "fine-sounding arguments."

Now or Later

Study Colossians 2:6-7 more closely. To learn more about the importance of strong roots, find information about growing trees and shrubs. Identify things that try to uproot you from your faith. Resolve to practice thankfulness to the point of overflowing!

Study John 15:1-17, in which Jesus says we can do nothing unless we continue in him, as a branch must remain connected to the vine.

Study 1 Corinthians 1:18-25, in which Paul calls Christ "the power of God and the wisdom of God."

3

Listening to the Young

Job 32

"Listen to your elders." When we're young, we don't want to hear it. When we're older, we say it ourselves, but by that time, who listens?

Once we have lived a certain number of years and accumulated a certain amount of experience, shouldn't younger people defer to us? Haven't we earned that right? Scripture does admonish the younger to respect the older. On the other hand, wisdom is not the automatic accompaniment of aging. Wisdom comes not from the calendar but from God the Creator.

GROUP DISCUSSION. When are you most likely to listen to guidance from a younger person? When are you least likely to listen? Give specific examples.

PERSONAL REFLECTION. How do you respond when a younger person approaches you to make a suggestion or to try to give advice? Do you think younger people find you easy or difficult to approach? Why?

In a short time Job endured a crushing series of disasters: he lost his material wealth, his children and his health. He was reduced to sitting on an ash heap. His own wife advised him to "curse God and die," but he did not blame God. Three friends who came to see Job insisted that he must have brought all this tragedy on himself through his own sin. Then a fourth visitor spoke up. *Read Job 32.*

1. Why did Elihu hesitate to speak out, and how did he overcome his reluctance (vv. 6-9)?

2. Does Elihu strike you as an admirable person or not? Why?

3. Elihu sat and listened for a long time as Job and his three friends conversed. What angered Elihu about the conversation (vv. 1-5)?

4. Why is age irrelevant to wisdom (vv. 8-9)?

5. Experience shows us that, as people grow older, some get wiser and some do not. What do you think makes the difference?

6. On what basis could Elihu demand that the older men now listen to him (vv. 10-14)?

7. When have you benefited from the wisdom of someone younger?

8. How did Elihu feel as he waited to speak out (vv. 15-22)?

9. What would safeguard him from insincerity in his speech (vv. 21-22)?

10. What evidence do you see that, though Job's elder friends had spoken from the knowledge of their years, they had failed to speak with the understanding that comes from God?

11. Where might you be rejecting the wisdom of younger people?

12. What steps will you take to listen more closely to younger believers who are wise beyond their years?

Pray that you will be increasingly open to that wisdom which comes only from God. Pray that you will recognize God's wisdom in whatever way it comes to you.

Now or Later

Look for ways to include the views of younger people—and younger people themselves—in your fellowship and ministry efforts.

Study Ecclesiastes 4:13-16. What do you learn about the relative values of wealth, wisdom, age and youth?

4

When the Kids Are Grownups Too

"Do American young people marry against their parents' wishes?" a Chinese student asked us with some concern. "For us, the opinion of parents is very important. We would not marry without the consent of our parents."

Most Americans would find themselves torn between two opinions. We believe that grown children should respect and listen to their parents, but we look down on adults who remain under the thumb of Mom or Dad. When our children become adults, how much should we expect them to continue to defer to us? And if that question isn't complex enough, what about our daughters-in-law or sons-in-law? What about younger people in general? Long before any of us faced these questions, Moses and his father-in-law, Jethro, confronted them under great pressure in a remote desert.

GROUP DISCUSSION. When do you freely voice your opinions to younger people, and when do you hesitate? Why?

PERSONAL REFLECTION. Think of a time when you offered advice to a younger person. Was it easy or difficult? If you were hesitant to speak out, why? Are you glad you spoke up? What happened as a result of your suggestions?

Under Moses' leadership, God had miraculously brought the enslaved Israelites out of Egypt. They reached the vicinity of Mount Sinai but had not yet received the Ten Commandments. Moses' Midianite wife and two sons had not accompanied him on the journey. Now his wife, sons and father-in-law arrive at the Hebrew camp. *Read Exodus 18.*

1. Where are the potential points of conflict in this story?

2. When you see a younger person making foolish or dangerous choices, what do you do?

3. What can you discern about the relationship between Moses and Jethro from verses 5-8?

4. How did Jethro respond to Moses' account of the Lord's miracles and guidance (vv. 9-12)?

5. What surprised Jethro the next day (vv. 13-15)?

6. Notice how long Jethro observed the situation before he said anything (v. 13). Was this the appropriate length of time? Why or why not?

7. Before he gave any advice, what effort did Jethro make to understand the situation—and Moses' perspective on the situation (vv. 14-15)?

8. Jethro finally gave a rather blunt evaluation of what Moses was doing (v. 17). What misgivings might have gone through Jethro's mind before he spoke?

When have you felt like this with your grown children?

9. How did Jethro make the case that his suggestions would be good for Moses and good for the people (vv. 18-23)?

10. How did Jethro affirm Moses' abilities, even while he advised Moses to let go of some responsibilities?

11. As a result of Jethro's visit, what changes were brought about for the Hebrew people and for Moses in particular (vv. 24-27)?

12. What spirit do you think prevailed between Jethro and Moses as Jethro left (v. 27)?

13. The good results of verses 25-27 are a credit to both Moses and Jethro. "Moses listened" (v. 24), and Jethro gave counsel worth listening to. What wisdom would you like to pass along to your grown children or other young people?

14. How can you voice your ideas in a manner that expresses confidence in God and in your audience?

Pray that you will be sensitive to people's feelings, even when you believe they are making big mistakes. Ask God for wisdom to know when to be silent and when to speak up.

Now or Later

Think of a younger person who is going the wrong way, but whom you hesitate to approach. Write a letter of advice to that person. Ask a neutral person to read what you have written and give you an honest critique of your tone. Rewrite your letter and consider mailing it or verbally delivering your opinions. Even if you choose not to share your suggestions now, note anything you learn in the process about how to approach a person engaged in self-destructive behavior.

Study 1 Samuel 2:12-36. Note that although Eli's sons were responsible for their own actions, God rebuked Eli for the way he had indulged them. Note also God's sovereignty at work behind the scenes. While Eli's sons carried on their sham priesthood, God was quietly raising up Samuel as a faithful prophet for Israel.

5

Wiser by Faith

Genesis 24:1-9

Now that I am back in my hometown, I am often startled to find myself in some spot, such as at my high school or church, where years ago I confidently spouted off my opinions. I realize now how little I knew then, and I wish I had listened more to God and less to my own drive for importance.

Wisdom does not automatically come with age. However, we *can* get wiser as we get older, if we tap into the eternal wisdom of God.

GROUP DISCUSSION. If you could go back twenty years, what is one thing you would do differently, and why?

PERSONAL REFLECTION. What has God taught you through mistakes you made years ago?

God had promised Abraham and Sarah a son in their old age. At Sarah's insistence, Abraham conceived a child with Sarah's maid Hagar. But the child was not the child of God's promise, and Abraham allowed Sarah to banish Hagar before their son Ishmael was born. Twice Abraham passed off Sarah as his sister to save his own life. After Sarah gave birth to Isaac, the child of promise, Abraham again banished Hagar along with Ishmael. Now, years later, Abraham desires to find a wife for Isaac. Has he learned anything about trusting the Lord in his family life? *Read Genesis 24:1-9.*

---

1. What do Abraham's instructions to his servant reveal about his most urgent concerns for his family?

---

2. Where do your concerns for your own family mesh with those of Abraham at this point in his life?

Where do your concerns differ from Abraham's?

---

3. Why do you think Abraham was determined to keep Isaac from marrying a Canaanite woman (vv. 1-4)?

---

4. How did Abraham allow for the prospective bride's choice in the matter (vv. 5-8)?

5. What were some of the dangers of letting Isaac return to Abraham's homeland (vv. 6-8)?

6. Where do you struggle to find a balance between exercising control over your family (or other younger people over whom you have some authority) and giving them freedom to make their own choices?

7. How did Abraham display a mature trust in God's purposes for him and his family (v. 7)?

8. How do you see God's purposes being fulfilled in the life of your family?

9. The servant agreed to faithfully follow Abraham's instructions (v. 9). Who has helped you carry out the purposes of God for yourself and other family members?

10. In this incident how did Abraham demonstrate his growing maturity, compared with his actions earlier in life?

11. If Abraham had not grown in his faith over the years, how do you think his story would be different at this point?

12. How would you like future chapters of your own story to reflect a growing dependence on the Lord?

Thank God for events in your life that have led to more maturity. Ask for insight into areas where your faith still needs to grow.

Now or Later

Consider how you can help mentor a younger person by sharing ways God has helped you become a more mature believer.

Study Titus 2:1-5, in which Paul writes that older people in the church should teach and set examples for younger believers.

6

They Don't
Always Listen

"I've told them and told them until I'm blue in the face, and they still don't listen." No, sometimes they don't. Then what do we do? If God did not exist or was not interested in us, then we would have no choice but despair. But God is here! And not only is he interested, he is committed to what is best for us. He works through circumstances and in people's hearts to accomplish his will, even when we don't see how it can be possible. Yet in the end, as much as we would like him to, God does not force his will on rebellious people.

GROUP DISCUSSION. In what situations do you look for intergenerational advice, and in what situations do you look for advice from your peers?

PERSONAL REFLECTION. Have you ever followed a suggestion simply because you knew and liked the person who suggested it? What happened as a result?

When King Solomon fell into idolatry, God chose Jeroboam, one of Solomon's most capable officials, to appropriate most of Solomon's kingdom. Jeroboam had to flee into exile until Solomon died and Solomon's son Rehoboam was made king. *Read 1 Kings 12:1-20.*

1. How did Rehoboam's two sources of counsel conflict with each other?

2. When you need guidance, do you usually go to one source you trust, or do you consult with several sources and then decide? Why?

3. How did Rehoboam show initial signs that he might be a judicious ruler (vv. 1-6)?

4. What gave credibility to the elders' advice (vv. 6-7)?

5. How did they make a case for the wisdom of their words?

6. Rehoboam had received sound guidance from wise people. Why do you think he rejected their advice and turned to his peers for a second opinion (vv. 8-9)?

7. What was the appeal of the younger men's advice (vv. 10-11)?

8. The older advisors refused to be "yes men," no doubt at some risk to themselves. Imagine that you overhear what they say to each other when they witness the events of verses 12-14. Quote some of their remarks.

9. When have you said or thought something similar?

10. The elders waited to offer advice until they were asked by Rehoboam (vv. 6-7). How would you decide when it is appropriate to give advice to a younger person who is going the wrong way, and when it is appropriate to back off and wait for God?

11. Rehoboam's decision to reject his elders' advice bore prompt and lasting political effects (vv. 16-20). What perspective does verse 15 bring to those events?

12. Where are you up against the stubbornness of a younger person?

13. In your situation, how might God be working out his purposes in the stubborn person?

in other people who are involved?

in you?

Pray for patience and understanding toward those who will not listen. Examine your own heart for pride or selfish ambition, which demands to be heard.

Now or Later

Recall times when you recklessly followed your peers and ignored the wisdom of an older person. Looking back from the perspective of today, how do you see God at work even in your close-minded attitude?

Study Ezekiel 3:1-11. God sent Ezekiel to give the people a message, even though God knew they would not listen. Consider what it means to be a faithful messenger no matter how others respond.

Read 1 Kings 12:21-24 to see how Rehoboam made his next decisions.

7

A Reason to Be Here

Philippians 1:18-26

I know some people who always look on the bright side. According to them, life is getting better every day; every cloud has a silver lining and prosperity is just around the corner. It's not surprising that most of these relentless optimists are young.

When we're young, we have time for optimism. The future looks like an endless canvas on which to paint life in any form we choose. If we don't accomplish something today, we can do it tomorrow, or next year, or next decade. As we get older, those future prospects compress themselves into fewer and fewer years. What if we don't have time to do everything we want to do or feel we should do?

In prison the apostle Paul did not know if God would grant him many more years or only a few more days. He became confident that God had a purpose for his remaining time on earth, whether short or long.

GROUP DISCUSSION. What do you hope people will remember about your life?

PERSONAL REFLECTION. Place an X on this optimism-pessimism

scale to mark your typical attitude toward life:

Gloomy Pessimist   Sunny Optimist

_____

What would you like to be more optimistic about?

Paul's letter to the Philippians is one of his prison letters. While Paul was imprisoned in Rome, the church at Philippi (which Paul had started) sent him a gift. Epaphroditus, who brought the gift, became ill in Rome and nearly died. Now he has recovered, and Paul sends him back to Philippi along with this warmhearted letter of thanks. *Read Philippians 1:18-26.*

_____

1. What were Paul's reasons for optimism?

_____

2. Does Paul's attitude surprise you, or do you think it is to be expected, and why?

_____

3. In verses 18-19, Paul sounds as though he anticipates release from prison. How does verse 20 change the dynamic of his situation?

4. We do not know Paul's age when he wrote this letter, but he was a person who faced the possibility that he would die in prison—perhaps sooner rather than later. How does his situation parallel that of a person who is aging?

5. What would have made Paul ashamed (v. 20)?

6. Consider Paul's desire to exalt Christ "whether by life or by death" (v. 20). How do you respond to the idea that it does not ultimately matter whether a person lives or dies?

7. What do you think Paul meant by "to live is Christ" (v. 21)?

8. For Paul what were the advantages of living and of dying (vv. 21-26)?

9. What overriding purpose did Paul see in his remaining alive (vv. 22-26)?

10. Whose "progress and joy in the faith" helps give you purpose for your remaining years in this life (v. 25)?

11. In the past several years, what is one way you have grown in your resolve to honor Christ?

12. What is one godly purpose that you have let slide in the past few years?

13. What steps will you take to renew your resolve to live in a way that honors Christ?

Offer praise that your life is not an aimless accident and that the Lord gives you purpose. Ask him to clarify his purposes for you in areas where you are uncertain—or perhaps overly certain.

Now or Later

Paul hoped that he would exalt Christ whether by life or by death. Have you known someone whose death glorified Christ? Tell or write about that person, especially how that person's life and death transformed

- your worship of Christ
- your attitude toward dying
- your attitude toward living

Second Timothy is the closest we have to Paul's last words; it is his last known writing. Study 2 Timothy 4:6-18, looking for answers to these questions: How had Paul's outlook changed since he wrote his letter to the Philippians? How had his outlook remained consistent?

8

Dealing with Fears

Psalm 71:1-13

Refugee. The word brings up images of desperate people lined up at border crossings, clutching a few possessions. Or perhaps we think of vast tent cities filled with sad-eyed children, surrounded by high wire fences. To be a refugee is to be without home or help.

But at the root, what is a refugee? It is one who has taken refuge. Regardless of our wealth or nationality, the Lord offers refuge to each of us. As we get older, we feel more and more of our need to take shelter in him.

GROUP DISCUSSION. What are some positives and some negatives about independence?

PERSONAL REFLECTION. When you think of aging, what do you fear most? What do you hope for most?

The writers of the Psalms faced the same fears we face, including the fear of weakness in old age. In this session we pick up the first part of the psalm—and in the next session we will complete it. *Read Psalm 71:1-13.*

1. Throughout this passage what is the significance of the word *refuge?*

2. When and how has the Lord proved to be a refuge for you?

3. How do past and future come together in verses 1-4?

4. The psalmist refers to the Lord as "my hope" and "my confidence" (v. 5). How does that differ from saying, "The Lord gives me hope," or "The Lord gives me confidence"?

5. In verses 5-8 the psalmist gives a very abbreviated version of his life history. How does his history resemble yours?

How does your history differ from the psalmist's?

6. Despite his confidence, what fears does the psalmist betray in verses 9-11?

7. What dangers do we become vulnerable to as we age?

8. How does the psalmist show that he still sees the Lord as his refuge (vv. 12-13)?

9. If you were the psalm writer, and you wrote verses 9-13 today, what would they say?

10. As you look at growing older, what resources do you count on most?

11. Where do you need to transfer more of your trust to the Lord?

Pray that no matter what happens, you will always take refuge in God.

Now or Later

Draw or sketch a picture that represents what you fear most about aging. Now draw something that represents a "refuge." Place yourself inside that refuge. Write a prayer to the Lord about your fears. Ask him to be your hope and confidence.

Study Luke 2:25-38. Simeon and Anna had grown wise as they contemplated the Lord and worshiped him. The Scripture does not specifically say that Simeon was old; it does say that God prolonged his life until he could see the Christ.

9

Lifelong Trust

Psalm 71:14-24

In the past few years we have lost three large oak trees at the edge of our woods. Each was a shock to me because the trees had "always" been there (in other words, during my lifetime). I am grateful that my favorite tree, a huge pin oak, still stands. I used to say casually that I hoped it never fell. Now I've changed that to "I hope it doesn't fall in my lifetime."

Like us, trees have a life span. Like us, they will all fall sometime, no matter how much we hope to the contrary. In order to have indestructible hope, we must place our hope in the eternal God.

GROUP DISCUSSION. How important is hope to a person's well-being? Why?

PERSONAL REFLECTION. When has God turned a hopeless situation into a hopeful one for you?

In study 8 you read the first half of a psalm by an older person who sought refuge in God. Now read the rest of his words in *Psalm 71:14-24.*

1. What were the psalmist's plans for the future?

2. Which of his plans are also your plans?

3. What particular intention of the psalmist runs through verses 14-18?

4. Why does the desire to tell our experiences become more urgent as we get older?

5. Who in the "next generation" (v. 18) do you especially want to tell about the Lord's faithfulness?

6. What role had trouble played in the psalmist's life (vv. 19-21)?

7. How do verses 20-21 reveal the writer's growing spiritual maturity?

8. What is the relationship between trouble and hope?

9. Consider the mood of verses 22-24. We would all like to have such an attitude at the last part of our lives. What clues do you find in these verses that tell you why the writer was able to keep up a joyful and hopeful spirit?

10. In what aspects of your life are you particularly confident in the Lord—that he is your hope and security?

11. In what aspects of your life do you long to experience more peace and confidence in the Lord?

As you complete this study, thank God for his faithfulness through the years. Ask him for the growing assurance that he will stay with you in the future and that you will spend eternity with him.

Now or Later

Draw a picture of hope—whatever "hope" looks like to you. Where is God in the picture? Revise the picture if necessary so your hope more closely resembles the hope of the writer of Psalm 71.

Study Psalm 92:12-15 and Isaiah 46:3-4, which assure us that God will sustain us through old age so that we continue to live useful lives for him.

Leader's Notes

MY GRACE IS SUFFICIENT FOR YOU. (2 COR 12:9)

Leading a Bible discussion can be an enjoyable and rewarding experience. But it can also be *scary*—especially if you've never done it before. If this is your feeling, you're in good company. When God asked Moses to lead the Israelites out of Egypt, he replied, "O LORD, please send someone else to do it" (Ex 4:13). It was the same with Solomon, Jeremiah and Timothy, but God helped these people in spite of their weaknesses, and he will help you as well.

You don't need to be an expert on the Bible or a trained teacher to lead a Bible discussion. The idea behind these inductive studies is that the leader guides group members to discover for themselves what the Bible has to say. This method of learning will allow group members to remember much more of what is said than a lecture would.

These studies are designed to be led easily. As a matter of fact, the flow of questions through the passage from observation to interpretation to application is so natural that you may feel that the studies lead themselves. This study guide is also flexible. You can use it with a variety of groups—student, professional, neighborhood or church groups. Each study takes forty-five to sixty minutes in a group setting.

There are some important facts to know about group dynamics and encouraging discussion. The suggestions listed below should enable you to effectively and enjoyably fulfill your role as leader.

Preparing for the Study

1. Ask God to help you understand and apply the passage in your

own life. Unless this happens, you will not be prepared to lead others. Pray too for the various members of the group. Ask God to open your hearts to the message of his Word and motivate you to action.

2. Read the introduction to the entire guide to get an overview of the entire book and the issues which will be explored.

3. As you begin each study, read and reread the assigned Bible passage to familiarize yourself with it.

4. This study guide is based on the New International Version of the Bible. It will help you and the group if you use this translation as the basis for your study and discussion.

5. Carefully work through each question in the study. Spend time in meditation and reflection as you consider how to respond.

6. Write your thoughts and responses in the space provided in the study guide. This will help you to express your understanding of the passage clearly.

7. It might help to have a Bible dictionary handy. Use it to look up any unfamiliar words, names or places. (For additional help on how to study a passage, see chapter five of *How to Lead a LifeGuide Bible Study,* InterVarsity Press.)

8. Consider how you can apply the Scripture to your life. Remember that the group will follow your lead in responding to the studies. They will not go any deeper than you do.

9. Once you have finished your own study of the passage, familiarize yourself with the leader's notes for the study you are leading. These are designed to help you in several ways. First, they tell you the purpose the study guide author had in mind when writing the study. Take time to think through how the study questions work together to accomplish that purpose. Second, the notes provide you with additional background information or suggestions on group dynamics for various questions. This information can be useful when people have difficulty understanding or answering a question. Third, the leader's notes can alert you to potential problems you may encounter during the study.

10. If you wish to remind yourself of anything mentioned in the leader's notes, make a note to yourself below that question in the study.

Leading the Study

1. Begin the study on time. Open with prayer, asking God to help the group to understand and apply the passage.

2. Be sure that everyone in your group has a study guide. Encourage the group to prepare beforehand for each discussion by reading the introduction to the guide and by working through the questions in the study.

3. At the beginning of your first time together, explain that these studies are meant to be discussions, not lectures. Encourage the members of the group to participate. However, do not put pressure on those who may be hesitant to speak during the first few sessions. You may want to suggest the following guidelines to your group.

■ Stick to the topic being discussed.

■ Your responses should be based on the verses which are the focus of the discussion and not on outside authorities such as commentaries or speakers.

■ These studies focus on a particular passage of Scripture. Only rarely should you refer to other portions of the Bible. This allows for everyone to participate in in-depth study on equal ground.

■ Anything said in the group is considered confidential and will not be discussed outside the group unless specific permission is given to do so.

■ We will listen attentively to each other and provide time for each person present to talk.

■ We will pray for each other.

4. Have a group member read the introduction at the beginning of the discussion.

5. Every session begins with a group discussion question. The question or activity is meant to be used before the passage is read. The question introduces the theme of the study and encourages group members to begin to open up. Encourage as many members as possible to participate, and be ready to get the discussion going with your own response.

This section is designed to reveal where our thoughts or feelings need to be transformed by Scripture. That is why it is especially important not to read the passage before the discussion question is asked. The passage will tend to color the honest reactions people would otherwise give because they are, of course, supposed to think the way the Bible does.

You may want to supplement the group discussion question with an icebreaker to help people to get comfortable. See the community section of *Small Group Idea Book* for more ideas.

You also might want to use the personal reflection question with your group. Either allow a time of silence for people to respond individually or discuss it together.

6. Have a group member (or members if the passage is long) read aloud the passage to be studied. Then give people several minutes to read the passage again silently so that they can take it all in.

7. Question 1 will generally be an overview question designed to briefly survey the passage. Encourage the group to look at the whole passage, but try to avoid getting sidetracked by questions or issues that will be addressed later in the study.

8. As you ask the questions, keep in mind that they are designed to be used just as they are written. You may simply read them aloud. Or you may prefer to express them in your own words.

There may be times when it is appropriate to deviate from the study guide. For example, a question may have already been answered. If so, move on to the next question. Or someone may raise an important question not covered in the guide. Take time to discuss it, but try to keep the group from going off on tangents.

9. Avoid answering your own questions. If necessary, repeat or rephrase them until they are clearly understood. Or point out something you read in the leader's notes to clarify the context or meaning. An eager group quickly becomes passive and silent if they think the leader will do most of the talking.

10. Don't be afraid of silence. People may need time to think about the question before formulating their answers.

11. Don't be content with just one answer. Ask, "What do the rest of you think?" or "Anything else?" until several people have given answers to the question.

12. Acknowledge all contributions. Try to be affirming whenever possible. Never reject an answer. If it is clearly off-base, ask, "Which

verse led you to that conclusion?" or again, "What do the rest of you think?"

13. Don't expect every answer to be addressed to you, even though this will probably happen at first. As group members become more at ease, they will begin to truly interact with each other. This is one sign of healthy discussion.

14. Don't be afraid of controversy. It can be very stimulating. If you don't resolve an issue completely, don't be frustrated. Move on and keep it in mind for later. A subsequent study may solve the problem.

15. Periodically summarize what the group has said about the passage. This helps to draw together the various ideas mentioned and gives continuity to the study. But don't preach.

16. At the end of the Bible discussion you may want to allow group members a time of quiet to work on an idea under "Now or Later." Then discuss what you experienced. Or you may want to encourage group members to work on these ideas between meetings. Give an opportunity during the session for people to talk about what they are learning.

17. Conclude your time together with conversational prayer, adapting the prayer suggestion at the end of the study to your group. Ask for God's help in following through on the commitments you've made.

18. End on time.

Many more suggestions and helps are found in *How to Lead a LifeGuide Bible Study.*

Components of Small Groups

A healthy small group should do more than study the Bible. There are four components to consider as you structure your time together.

Nurture. Small groups help us to grow in our knowledge and love of God. Bible study is the key to making this happen and is the foundation of your small group.

Community. Small groups are a great place to develop deep friendships with other Christians. Allow time for informal interaction before and after each study. Plan activities and games that will help you get to know each other. Spend time having fun together—going on a picnic or cooking dinner together.

Worship and prayer. Your study will be enhanced by spending time praising God together in prayer or song. Pray for each other's needs—and keep track of how God is answering prayer in your group. Ask God to help you to apply what you are learning in your study.

Outreach. Reaching out to others can be a practical way of applying what you are learning, and it will keep your group from becoming self-focused. Host a series of evangelistic discussions for your friends or neighbors. Clean up the yard of an elderly friend. Serve at a soup kitchen together, or spend a day working on a Habitat house.

Many more suggestions and helps in each of these areas are found in *Small Group Idea Book.* Information on building a small group can be found in *Small Group Leaders' Handbook* and *The Big Book on Small Groups* (both from InterVarsity Press). Reading through one of these books would be worth your time.

Study 1. Wise Up! James 1:1-8, 12.

Purpose: To desire godly wisdom.

Question 2. "The call to rejoice, however, is not masochistic. Masochism is taking pleasure in pain. The masochist wants to experience pain because it is the pain that gives this person pleasure. In these passages, however, we are not to rejoice in the pain, but in the future reward beyond the pain. James believes we should rejoice because trials give us an opportunity to develop the virtue of perseverance, which will in turn lead to a mature Christian character. We rejoice like an athlete in a practice session. Athletes may run or lift weights to the point of pain, but all the time their eyes are set on the big race or game. They rejoice not in the enjoyment of the stress but in the knowledge that their muscles are growing stronger and therefore they will do better when it counts" (Walter C. Kaiser Jr. et al., *Hard Sayings of the Bible* [Downers Grove, Ill.: InterVarsity Press, 1996], pp. 693-94).

Question 3. Because wisdom follows perseverance in the text, it may appear that perseverance leads to wisdom. However, James tells his readers that if they lack wisdom, they should ask God. He implies that wisdom is necessary to sustain perseverance. Matthew Henry wrote, "When the work of patience is complete, it will furnish all that is necessary for our Christian race and warfare. We should not pray so much for the removal of affliction, as for wisdom to make a right use of it. And who does not want wisdom to guide him under trials, both in regulating his own spirit, and in managing his affairs?" (*Matthew Henry's Commentary on the Whole Bible, Condensed Version*, Sage Digital Library [Albany, Ore.: Sage Software, 1996], p. 1654).

Question 5. "The Greek term for 'mature' is also often translated as 'perfect'. This is the virtue that Noah exhibited in Gn. 6:9 (translated 'blameless' in the NIV). This is what Jesus intends when he calls his followers to be 'perfect, therefore, as your heavenly Father is perfect' (Mt. 5:48). It indicates a character like God's. This type of maturity is produced by holding fast to the faith and Christian virtue while in the fire of persecution. The impurities in one's character will be burned off. The end result will be not just maturity, but completeness, which means that not a single part of a God-like character will be lacking. If this is the end result of the readers' trials, difficult as they may be, there is indeed something to rejoice about" (G. J. Wenham et al., eds., *New Bible Commentary* [Downers Grove, Ill.: InterVarsity Press, 1994], p. 1357).

Questions 7, 9. "Yet there is one requirement if we are to receive wisdom: the asking must flow out of faith in, or rather commitment to, God. The 'doubting' James warns about is not that of a person who wonders whether or not God will answer this particular request, or that of an introspective doubter who struggles with faith. Instead it is that of a person who is *double-minded* . . . the person who is not wholly committed to God, but 'plays safe' by praying. Their real interest is in advancement in this world, but they also want to enjoy some of God's blessings now and go to heaven when they die. Such a person will not get wisdom, James says. In fact, such a person will not receive anything at all from God" (Wenham et al., *New Bible Commentary,* p. 1356).

Question 8. The doubt of verse 6 is not so much uncertainty about God's answer as it is double-mindedness (v. 8), when the person who prays really wants something else besides that which would please God.

Study 2. Wisdom Hunt. Colossians 2:1-10.

Purpose: To search for wisdom in the right place—with God.

Question 1. Notice the contrasts Paul draws: between being encouraged and being deceived (vv. 2-3), between continuing in Christ and being taken captive (vv. 6-8). "The purpose of his [Paul's] apostolic activity was that their lives might be strengthened. *United in love* suggests that as love binds them all together so they would attain to full understanding and knowledge. But the verb could mean 'instructed'. . . . Since the context emphasizes knowledge and wisdom, and Paul was less concerned about the need for the Colossians' unity than their instruction in the faith over against false teaching, 'taught' or 'instructed' is better" (Wenham et al., *New Bible Commentary,* p. 1268).

Question 3. Paul no doubt uses *mystery* as a word play with those who sought to deceive the Colossians through "the sacred rites [and teachings] of the Gk. mystery religions in which only the initiated shared" (S. S. Smalley, "Mystery," in *New Bible Dictionary,* 3rd ed., ed. I. Howard Marshall et al. [Leicester, England: Inter-Varsity Press, 1996], p. 794). Paul counters their deception by writing that the true mystery of God is "Christ, in whom are hidden all the treasures of wisdom and knowledge" (Col 2:2).

Question 4. "Probably with a side-glance at the false teaching Paul encourages the readers to look to Christ as the only 'place' where these *treasures of wisdom* are available. *Hidden* does not mean 'concealed' but 'deposited' or 'stored up' (*cf.* 1:26). To search for other sources of knowledge apart from Christ is useless" (Wenham et al., *New Bible Commentary,* p. 1268).

Questions 9-10. "Stoics spoke of the deity as being filled by all things, usually in a pantheistic sense; Greek-speaking Jewish writers modified this language to refer to God's rule encompassing all things. . . . Whatever precise sense Paul means by 'fullness,' he clearly means that access to all that God is and does is available only through Christ, a function ancient Judaism often attributed to divine Wisdom" (Craig S. Keener, *The IVP Bible Background Commentary: New Testament* [Downers Grove, Ill.: InterVarsity Press, 1993], p. 575).

Study 3. Listening to the Young. Job 32.

Purpose: To discern and welcome the wisdom of younger believers.

Question 1. "Elihu confesses he is young and he voices his respect for the wisdom of age (6-7), but he has taken courage from his belief that all are created with an equal capacity for wisdom (8). Therefore it is not only the old that are wise (9). So he is not afraid to declare *what I know* (10). He has also been encouraged to enter the conversation by the feebleness of the friends' speeches (11-12). It seems to Elihu that they are rather overwhelmed by Job's arguments and are starting to think that only God can refute him (13)" (Wenham et al., *New Bible Commentary*, p. 478).

Question 3. "The young Elihu is obviously very *angry* (the word is repeated four times in vs 2, 3, 5; one of the occurrences in v 2 is omitted by the NIV). He is angry at Job because he had 'made himself out to be more righteous than God' (2; NEB). This is a much more serious criticism than appears in the NIV, which has him *justifying himself rather than God*. Elihu means that the logic of Job's claim, that he is in the right in his dispute with God, is that God must be in the wrong. Job had never said exactly that, but it is a reasonable conclusion. Elihu is also angry at the three friends because they *found no way to refute Job* (3), *i.e.* they had been unable to convince Job that God was not in the wrong"(Wenham et al., *New Bible Commentary*, p. 478).

Question 8. "New wineskins are able to endure fermenting wine, since the skins expand along with the wine. If the wineskins are bottled up in this process, they are in danger of exploding, unless they are vented" (John H. Walton, Victor H. Matthews and Mark W. Chavalas, eds., *The IVP Bible Background Commentary: Old Testament* [Downers Grove, Ill.: InterVarsity Press, 2000], p. 508).

Question 9. The temptation to flatter others and show partiality is common to all human relationships, and it kills sincerity. Elihu's protection against insincerity is his awareness that he must answer to God for what he says.

Study 4. When the Kids Are Grownups Too. Exodus 18.

Purpose: To develop the courage to speak up and give advice with godly wisdom.

Question 1. The members of this family are from different cultural backgrounds with different expectations. As head of his family, Jethro was used to being in charge; Moses had served him as his son-in-law, and he was a priest among his own people. On the other hand, Moses had been chosen by God to lead the Israelites, he had witnessed the overthrow of the Egyptian Pharaoh, and he now held his own powerful position of leadership. The meeting of two strong leaders with different backgrounds is loaded with potential conflict.

Question 3. "Moses' greeting of Jethro follows standard practice. Bowing down is a greeting to one who is of higher social standing and is an act of respect. The kiss on the cheek is the greeting of friendship. This is the only recorded incident where both are performed" (Walton, Matthews and Chavalas, *Bible Background Commentary: OT*, p. 93). It was natural for Moses to share the good news of all God had done, in order to bring Jethro up to date on what had happened since they last met.

Question 4. "Jethro's acknowledgment of the superiority of Yahweh does not suggest that he was a worshiper of Yahweh or that he became a worshiper of Yahweh. The polytheism of the ancient world allowed for the recognition of the relative strengths of various deities" (Walton, Matthews and Chavalas, *Bible Background Commentary: OT*, p. 93).

Question 8. Jethro might have thought of things like: "Moses is God's chosen leader; I shouldn't say anything; He's known as a hothead. What if he threatens me? My daughter will be mad at me if I say anything. It's not my place to criticize. He'll probably change while I'm here and then go back to his old ways after I leave, so why bother?"

Question 9. Jethro first pointed out that both the people and Moses would be worn out with the present system. He affirmed Moses' rightful place in teaching the people how to live. He then suggested that Moses appoint capable men to share the burden by deciding the easier cases. "Jethro advises Moses to establish a hierarchical judiciary with Moses at the top, as a king would have been in a monarchy, and as a priest or family patriarch would have been in tribal societies. In this structure some disputes can be settled . . . in the lower levels. In the absence of sufficient evidence in complex or serious cases, the matter was handled 'prophetically'—that is, it was brought before God. This was where Moses' involvement was essential" (Walton, Matthews and Chavalas, *Bible Background Commentary: OT,* p. 93).

Study 5. Wiser by Faith. Genesis 24:1-9.

Purpose: To exercise trust in God in our dealings with family.

Question 1. Remember that Abraham had been promised that through Isaac he would be the father of a great nation more numerous than the stars of heaven or the sand of the sea. "As befits a man who had given his life to fulfilling promises, Abraham's last words expressed his concern that this should also be the family's priority after he had gone. He made his servant swear to find Isaac a wife, a prerequisite if the promise of numerous descendants was to be realized. She must not be a Canaanite but come from Abraham's relatives and, like Abraham, be willing to settle in Canaan (5-9)" (Wenham et al., *New Bible Commentary,* p. 76).

Questions 2-3. "The practice of marrying within one's own tribe or family is called endogamy. Endogamy could be the result of religious, social or ethnic concerns. In this text it appears to be ethnic in that there are no suggestions that the family of Laban, Rebekah and Rachel shares the religious beliefs of Abraham and his family. . . . In this text the endogamy seems motivated by the covenant that seeks to prevent Abraham and his family from simply being assimilated into the ethnic melting pot in Canaan" (Walton, Matthews and Chavalas, *Bible Background Commentary: OT,* p. 55).

Question 5. Probably the two greatest dangers were that Isaac might decide to stay in the land that God had told Abraham to leave (Gen 12:1) and that Isaac would abandon God and return to the religious practices of his ancestors.

Question 10. Notice how much of the situation Abraham leaves in God's hands (vv. 7-8), in contrast to his previous maneuvers of fleeing to Egypt to escape famine, calling Sarah his sister to protect his life and taking Hagar as a concubine to provide the heir God had promised.

Study 6. They Don't Always Listen. 1 Kings 12:1-20.

Purpose: To trust God's purposes even when people we care about are headed the wrong way.

Question 3. "At first Rehoboam seems to act prudently. He makes no immediate response, but takes three days to consult his advisors" (Wenham et al., *New Bible Commentary,* p. 350). We should not imagine that Rehoboam was an impulsive teen. According to 1 Kings 14:21, he was forty-one years old when he began to reign.

Question 4. "The 'elders' would represent those who had been in office during the time of Solomon. They may have come either from the royal family (half brothers, cousins like Jonadab in 2 Sam 13:3) or the civil service" (Walton, Matthews and Chavalas, *Bible Background Commentary: OT,* p. 432). Their years of service would give them the experience to predict the people's response to Rehoboam's reply to their request.

Question 5. The elders' advice that Rehoboam should be a servant to the people (v. 7) is much like Jesus' words to his disciples when they argued about who would be the greatest: "Whoever wants to become great among you must be your servant, and whoever wants to be first must be slave of all" (Mk 10:43-44).

Question 6. If group members are slow to respond, it may help to remind them of their answers to the group discussion question.

Question 7. Human nature is attracted to the appeal of power over servanthood. Group members may come up with other ideas.

Question 11. Second Chronicles 12:1 concisely states what happened as soon as Rehoboam was established as king: he and the entire nation abandoned the Lord! For the word God spoke to Jeroboam through the prophet Ahijah (v. 15), see 1 Kings 11:29-39. The sovereignty of God is obvious in this passage, which raises the question of why God would arrange matters so that the leader and people abandon him. However, "we must distinguish between foreordination and causality. God foreordains all things and he is the cause of many things, but not of *all* things" (D. Macleod, "Sovereignty," in *New Dictionary of Theology,* ed. Sinclair B. Ferguson and David F. White [Downers Grove, Ill.: InterVarsity Press, 1988], p. 655).

Study 7. A Reason to Be Here. Philippians 1:18-26.

Purpose: To be assured that God has his purposes for our lives no matter how many or few years we have on earth.

Question 1. "Paul faced imprisonment and the threat of death and, from fellow-Christians, animosity and provocation, and yet he was confident that all would turn out well (*cf.* Rom. 8:28). Humanly speaking he relied on the prayers of his friends, and in answer to them the unfailing help of the Holy Spirit. The Greek word translated *help* indicates both a generous provision and an undergirding strength. The assurance of *deliverance* is of the kind described in 2 Tim. 4:18, 'The Lord will rescue me from every evil attack and will bring me safely to his heavenly kingdom' " (Wenham et al., *New Bible Commentary*, p. 1250).

Question 3. "The word translated *eagerly expect* means straining forward with outstretched head, and its prepositional prefix implies a turning aside from all other interests. Paul has one supreme ambition: that Christ might be *exalted* in his *body*, living or dying; that Christ might be seen by others more clearly and in his true greatness" (Wenham et al., *New Bible Commentary*, p. 1250).

Question 5. Remember that Paul was held in prison, even in chains, which he said had given others greater courage to preach the gospel (Phil 1:12-13). When Paul wrote to the Ephesians, he specifically asked for their prayers that he would "fearlessly make known the mystery of the gospel" (Eph 6:19).

Questions 8-9. "The apostle's difficulty was not between living in this world and living in heaven; between these two there is no comparison; but between serving Christ in this world and enjoying him in another. Not between two evil things, but between two good things; living to Christ and being with him. See the power of faith and of Divine grace; it can make us willing to die. In this world we are compassed with sin; but when with Christ, we shall escape sin and temptation, sorrow and death, for ever. But those who have most reason to desire to depart, should be willing to remain in the world as long as God has any work for them to do" (*Matthew Henry's Commentary*, p. 1576).

Study 8. Dealing with Fears. Psalm 71:1-13.

Purpose: To put confidence in God for all stages of life.

General note. If group members feel frustrated at cutting Psalm 71 short, assure them that they will study the rest of the psalm in the next session.

Question 1. "No author is named for this psalm. There are Davidic expressions (e.g. 'my rock and my fortress'; 'my enemies'; 'make haste!'), but as the writer is drawing freely on earlier psalms this tells us little. All that we know, or need to know, is that he is old or aging, and has seen exceptional trouble (7) which shows no sign of abating. Against his failing strength he now sets a long memory of God's faithfulness and a growing hope in his life-renewing power" (Derek Kidner, *Psalms 1—72*, Tyndale Old Testament Commentary [Downers Grove, Ill.: InterVarsity Press, 1973], p. 250).

"The idea of 'refuge' in the OT may be traced back to the language of warfare—the 'secure heights' and the 'strong rock,' etc., describe both natural and artificial protection afforded by the rocky landscape of Canaan's mountain regions. . . . Refuge as an epithet of Yahweh is one of many synonymous expressions describing him as protector of men" (J. A. Wharton, "Refuge," in *Interpreter's Dictionary of the Bible,* ed. George A. Buttrick et al., vol. 4 [Nashville: Abingdon, 1962], p. 24).

Question 4. We might feel a general sense of hope that things will work out for the best and thank the Lord for that hope, but to say that the Lord *is* our hope is to express confidence in him no matter what happens.

Question 5. "The use of the Hebrew term *mopet* ["portent" in v. 7] is indicative of an extraordinary event that serves as a sign of God's power, and in this case judgment or punishment (compare the curses in Deut 28:45-46). This technical term appears often in the narrative of the plagues in Egypt (Ex 7:3; 11:9) and is used to signal a coming event (1 Kings 13:3, 5)" (Walton, Matthews and Chavalas, *Bible Background Commentary: OT*, p. 539).

Questions 6-7. Augustine, bishop of Hippo (A.D. 354-430), wrote of the psalmist's words in v. 9: "What is this time of old age? 'When my strength shall fail, forsake Thou not me.' Here God maketh this answer to thee, yea indeed let thy strength fail, in order that in thee mine may abide: in order that thou mayest say with the Apostle, 'When I am made weak, then I am mighty.' Fear not, that thou be cast away in that weakness, in that old age. But why? Was not thy Lord made weak on the Cross? . . . What did He hanging teach thee, that would not come down, but patience amid men reviling, but that thou shouldest be strong in thy God?" (Philip Schaff, ed., *Exposition on the Book of Psalms,* Sage Digital Library [Albany, Ore.: Sage Software, 1996], pp. 697-98).

Question 8. "David prays that he might never be made ashamed of dependence upon God. With this petition every true believer may come boldly to the throne of grace. The gracious care of Divine providence in our birth and infancy, should engage us to early piety. He that was our Help from our birth, ought to be our Hope from our youth. Let none expect ease or comfort from the world. Those who love the Lord, often are hated and persecuted; men wondered at for their principles and conduct; but the Lord has been their strong refuge. The faithful servants of God may be assured that he will not cast them off in old age, nor forsake them when their strength fails" (*Matthew Henry's Commentary,* p. 730).

Study 9. Lifelong Trust. Psalm 71:14-24.

Purpose: To enjoy the hope of trusting in the Lord for the remainder of life.

Question 1. While David must have been aware of the security that wealth and position would buy for him, his chief aim for the future was to continue to honor the Lord and to be sure that he communicated the Lord's faithfulness to future generations. Certainly David had no illusions about earthly security. He had seen his predecessor King Saul brought down (1 Sam 31), had fallen into great moral sin himself (2 Sam 11—12) and had seen his kingdom threatened numerous times, most dramatically by his son Absalom's rebellion (2 Sam 15—19).

Questions 3-4. As a follow-up question, ask group members to recall older people they have known who liked to tell the same stories over and over. Do they now have a better appreciation of why those people felt the urgency to tell those stories?

Question 6. Note that David apparently saw troubles not as an interruption of God's blessings in his life but as a necessary part of his spiritual growth.

Question 9. "The psalm opened with prayer (1-3); in 12-16 prayer merged into praise. Now only praise remains—for God's faithfulness, holiness, redemption, *righteous acts* (lit. 'righteousness', see 2, 15) and answered prayer (22-24, *cf.* 13). To this exercise of praise David brings his fingers to play, his lips to sing, and his tongue to tell" (Wenham et al., *New Bible Commentary*, p. 530).

Dale and Sandy Larsen are freelance writers living in Greenville, Illinois. They have authored over thirty Bible study guides, including the LifeGuide® Bible Studies Hosea: God's Persistent Love, Faith: Depending on God *and* Couples of the Old Testament.

What should we study next?

We have LifeGuides for . . .

LifeGuide® BIBLE STUDIES

KNOWING JESUS
Advent of the Savior
Following Jesus
I Am
Abiding in Christ
Jesus' Final Week

KNOWING GOD
Listening to God
Meeting God
God's Comfort
God's Love
The 23rd Psalm
Miracles

GROWING IN THE SPIRIT
Meeting the Spirit
Fruit of the Spirit
Spiritual Gifts
Spiritual Warfare

**LOOKING AT
THE TRINITY**
Images of Christ
Images of God
Images of the Spirit

**DEVELOPING
DISCIPLINES**
Christian Disciplines
God's Word
Hospitality
The Lord's Prayer
Prayer

Praying the Psalms
Sabbath
Worship

**DEEPENING
YOUR DOCTRINE**
Angels
Apostles' Creed
Christian Beliefs
The Cross
End Times
Good & Evil
Heaven
The Kingdom of God
The Story of Scripture

SEEKERS
Encountering Jesus
Jesus the Reason
Meeting Jesus

LEADERS
Christian Leadership
Integrity
Elijah
Joseph

**SHAPING YOUR
CHARACTER**
Christian Character
Decisions
Self-Esteem
Parables
Pleasing God

Woman of God
*Women of the
   New Testament*
*Women of the
   Old Testament*

**LIVING FULLY
AT EVERY STAGE**
Singleness
Marriage
Parenting
*Couples of the
   Old Testament*
*Couples of the
   New Testament*
*Growing Older
   & Wiser*

**REACHING
OUR WORLD**
Missions
Evangelism
Four Great Loves
Loving Justice

LIVING YOUR FAITH
Busyness
Christian Virtues
Forgiveness

**GROWING IN
RELATIONSHIPS**
Christian Community
Friendship

Find the perfect study for your group with IVP's LifeGuide Finder:
ivpress.com/lifeguidefinder